THE CLAIM

A play
By Tim Cowbury

First performed at The Crucible Theatre, Sheffield, on 22nd November 2017, as part of a UK tour, with the following cast:

SERGE	**Ncuti Gatwa**
A	**Nick Blakeley**
B	**Yusra Warsama**

Director	**Mark Maughan**
Set Designer	**Emma Bailey**
Sound Designer	**Lewis Gibson**
Lighting Designer	**Joshua Pharo**
Producer	**Luke Emery**
Engagement Producer	**Rhea Lewis**
Production Manager	**Louise Gregory**
Stage Manager	**Fana Sunley-Smith**
Casting Director	**Sophie Parrot CDG**
Associate Dramaturg	**Nick Walker**
Assistant Director	**Natasha Hyman**
Design Associate	**Natalie Parsons**

Developed with support from Arts Council England, GRAMNet, Old Vic New Voices, LUSH Charity Pot, ARC Stockton, Nuffield Southampton, Shoreditch Town Hall, Counterpoints Arts, MSN Fund.

COUNTERPOINTS ARTS

 University *of* Glasgow Glasgow Refugee, Asylum and Migration Network

Supported using public funding by
ARTS COUNCIL ENGLAND
LOTTERY FUNDED

 SHOREDITCH TOWN HALL

Creative Team

Tim Cowbury (Writer)

Tim is a playwright and theatre-maker. As co-founder of Made In China, he has created acclaimed works that have been performed across UK, Europe and USA. These include *Get Stuff Break Free* (National Theatre) *Tonight I'm Gonna Be The New Me* (Soho Theatre/UK tour) and *Double Double Act* (Unicorn Theatre). Tim's solo writing has been staged at Young Vic, Soho Theatre, Bush Theatre and The Public Theater (NYC). Current collaborations include projects with composer Tom Parkinson, director Tarek Iskander, and live artist/singer Livia Rita. Tim regularly leads workshops at schools, theatres and universities and has an MA in Writing For Performance (Goldsmiths University /AHRC scholarship).

Mark Maughan (Director)

Mark Maughan is a theatre director, maker and translator with a special interest in developing ideas with artists from the early stages of a project. Recently: recipient of Artists International Development Fund from the British and Arts Council; awarded Jerwood Choreographic Research Project II with Dan Daw; directing mentor to Tamir Theatre company in Ukraine via British Council, on their radical adaptation of *The Pitmen Painters* by Lee Hall; wrote/directed National Portrait Gallery's choral audio guide commission, read by Simon Russell Beale; *Open Plan* by Marcelo Dos Santos, a new commission at Royal Welsh College of Music and Drama; director of inaugural UK tour of *Petrification* by Zoe Cooper.

Emma Bailey (Set Designer)

Emma was awarded the prestigious Linbury Prize for Stage Design 2011 with her design for *Roy Orbison in Clingfilm* at the Royal Opera House. She has designed for various venues including Royal Opera House, Young Vic, RSC and National Theatre Studio. Check out more info on her website www.emmabaileydesigner.com

Lewis Gibson (Sound Designer)

Lewis designs sound and composes music for performance and other interventions. He is an associate member of Uninvited Guests, associate artist with Graeae Theatre and a founding member of the international touring company SABAB. Other theatre collaborations include Complicité / National Theatre, The Young Vic, The Place, Nigel and Louise, Made In China, Tim Crouch, Fuel, RET, Battersea Arts Centre, Berlin/Nevada and Cardboard Citizens. As a writer and director he has made a number of pieces of young people's theatre with The Royal Exchange, Tangere Arts, Fuel and The Unicorn.

Joshua Pharo (Lighting Designer)
Joshua works as a Lighting and Projection Designer across theatre, dance, opera, music, film & art installation. He was nominated for Knight of Illumination Award 2017 for *Removal Men*. Current/forthcoming projects include: *How I Hacked My Way Into Space* (UnLimited Theatre, Tour); *La Tradegie De Carmen* (Royal Opera House, Wilton's Music Hall); *Trust* (Gate Theatre). Recent credits include: *Frau Welt* (Hackney Showroom); *Cosmic Scallies* (Royal Exchange & Graeae); *Bullish* (Milk Presents); *The Shape of Pain* (China Plate Theatre; Fringe First Winner); *Burning Doors* (Belarus free Theatre); *Bodies* (Royal Court); *Nest* (Brighton & Take Off Festivals); *How My Light is Spent* (Royal Exchange); *The Bear and The Proposal* (Young Vic); *Scarlett* (Hampstead and Theatr Clywd).

Luke Emery (Producer)
Luke is an independent creative producer who works with artists and organisations that challenge and excite their audiences and who aren't afraid to ask difficult questions. He works outdoors, indoors, online and across the globe, wherever art can happen. Luke is the producer for Jamie Wood, Javaad Alipoor, Submerge Festival and Mayfest Radio. He has lectured and sat on panels on producing, sustainable working practices and project management for University of Bristol, Norwich University of the Arts, Derby University and Bath Spa University. He has produced projects for Situations & Theaster Gates, Mayfest, Norfolk & Norwich Festival, Yorkshire Festival and a wide range of independent artists.

Rhea Lewis (Engagement Producer)
Rhea collaborates with artists and with communities to create socially-engaged cross art-form creative projects and performances. Rhea has worked with diverse organisations, festivals and institutions such as The Work Room, A Moment's Peace Theatre Company, Tramway, Africa in Motion Film Festival, Glasgow Museums, The Arches and Untitled Projects. Currently, Rhea is co-founder of Glasgow based artist collective Project X, which champions dances of the African Diaspora in Scotland through workshops, professional development, symposium, performances and more. www.projectxplatform.co.uk

Fana Sunley-Smith (Stage Manager)
Fana is a Stage Manager based in London who works mainly on devised work; new writing; improvised and site specific projects. Highlights: *Opening Skinner's Box* (Lincoln Center NYC, 2017), *Connections Festival* (National Theatre); The Lounge (Soho, 2017); *Lost Without Words* by Improbable (National Theatre, 2017); *Christmas Cracker* (Ambassadors, 2016); *Everything By My Side* (Southbank Centre, 2016); *Opening Skinners Box* (Northern Stage, 2016); *Trois Ruptures* (The Print Room, 2015); *Have Your Circumstances Changed?* (Artangel, 2015); *All I Want* (Live Theatre, 2014); *How To Be Immortal* (2014), *A Beginning, a middle and an end* (Traverse, 2013); *Mass-Observation* (Almeida, 2012).

Louise Gregory (Production Manager)
Louise works as a Production and Stage Manager, and Lighting and Sound Designer. Recent credits include Production Manager for *salt* with Selina Thompson, *The Siege of Christmas* for Contact Young Company/Slung Low, and *The Believers Are But Brothers* with Javaad Alipoor; Company Stage Manager for Scamp Theatre's production of *Stick Man*; Lighting Designer for the butoh dance performance *Project Godie* for Surface Area Dance Theatre Company; and Sound Designer and Stage Manager for *Blackout* for Bunbury Banter Theatre Company.

Sophie Parrott CDG
Theatre includes: Company 2018 (Everyman); *An Octoroom* (Orange Tree); *All The President's Men?* (National Theatre); *This Beautiful Future* (Yard); *Death Of A Salesman* (Royal & Derngate); *Wish List* (Royal Court); *A Streetcar Named Desire* (co-casting, Royal Exchange); *Bird* (Sherman Cymru & Royal Exchange); *Yen* (Royal Court); *My Mother Said I Never Should* (St James); *Britannia Waves the Rules* (Tour); *A Midsummer Night's Dream* (Everyman); *The Crocodile* (MIF); *Billy Liar* (Royal Exchange). As Casting Associate, television includes: *Howard's End*, *Delicious*, *Rillington Place*, *Thirteen*, *Call the Midwife*, *Silent Witness*, *The Game*, *Esio Trot*, *Mr Stink*, *WPC56*, *The Night Watch*, *Holby City*, *The Riots: In Their Own Words*. As Casting Director, television includes: *Doctors*. www.sophieparrottcasting.com

Nick Walker (Associate Dramaturg)
Nick is a writer and director who has worked with some of the country's leading new work theatre companies and regional Reps. He has written over 30 plays and short stories for BBC Radio 4, including *The King of Mars*, with Peter Capaldi, and 3 series of *Annika Stranded*, starring Nicola Walker and is director of independent radio company Top Dog. He is the author of two critically acclaimed novels *Blackbox* and *Helloland* and was co-founder of Talking Birds, a Coventry-based theatre company. Nick was recently the Director of The Core at Corby Cube.

Natasha Hyman (Assistant Director)
Natasha trained on the MFA Theatre Directing at Birkbeck College, University of London. She was Trainee Director at West Yorkshire Playhouse 2016-7, assisting on *The Graduate* (including tour), *Pygmalion* (co-production with Headlong), *The Witches* (co-production with Curve) and *Sleuth* (co-production with Nottingham Playhouse). Direction includes *Ode to Leeds* by Zodwa Nyoni, rehearsed reading for Furnace Festival (West Yorkshire Playhouse), *M* by Alan Fielden for The Daily Plays produced by Etch and Squint (Pleasance, London) and *5 Encounters on a Site Called Craigslist* by Sam Ward for Live 1 curated by Barrel Organ (Camden Peoples' Theatre).

Natalie Parsons (Design Associate)
Natalie's designs include *One Minute* (Vaults), *Albee Vector the Sound Collector* (Arcola and tour), *Nabucco* (Newbury Corn Exchange), Carter Staged (White Bear). Music video and film designs include Rapunzel (Marine), How to Recognise a Work of Art (Meilyr Jones), Kickbox Hijabi (Alnoor Dewshi).

Ncuti Gatwa (Serge)
Ncuti is a Stage and Screen actor. Theatre credits include *Victoria*; *Hecuba*; *The BFG*; *And Then There Were None*; *Cars and Boys*; *Women in Mind* (Dundee Rep); *Romeo and Juliet* (Home, Manchester); *Shakespeare In Love* (West End); *946: The Amazing Story of Adolphus Tips* (Kneehigh/ Shakespeare's Globe); *Lines* (Yard Theatre); *A Midsummer Night's Dream* (Shakespeare's Globe); *Trouble in Mind* (Coronet Print Rooms). His TV credits include *Bob Servant* (BBC Scotland) and *Stonemouth* (BBC).

Nick Blakeley (A)
Nick trained at Bristol University and The Bristol Old Vic Theatre School. Theatre includes *Twelfth Night* (Orange Tree Theatre); *I Heart Catherine Pistachio* (Soho Theatre / Yard Theatre); *Brideshead Revisited* (York Theatre Royal / UK Tour); *Hapgood* (Hampstead Theatre); *Comment Is Free* (Old Vic Theatre); *The Last of the De Mullins* (Jermyn St Theatre); *And Other Stories* (Orange Tree Theatre); *Hard Feelings* (Finborough Theatre); *Happy Never After* (Pleasance Edinburgh); *The Sunshine Boys* (Savoy Theatre); *13, A Woman Killed With Kindness* (National Theatre). TV includes *Theresa Vs Boris: How May Became PM* (BBC); *Beyond Reasonable Doubt* (CNN); *Doctors* (BBC); and *The Old Bailey* (BBC). Film includes *Goodbye Christopher Robin* (Fox Searchlight) and *Eyes and Prize* (Independent Film).

Yusra Warsama (B)
Yusra Warsama is an Actor for Stage and Screen. Theatre Credits include *Corporation Street* (Home Theatre Manchester); *Shared Memories* and *Everybody Watches TV* (Contact Theatre Manchester); New Writing Festival (The Curve); *Bulletproof Soul* (Birmingham Rep); *Two Tone* (West Yorkshire Playhouse); *Bolt-Hole* and *Three Way* (Birmingham Rep); *Carri Mi Ackee* (Expression Dance); *Exposed* (Apples & Snakes); *Grace* and *Make Believe* (Quarantine). TV and Film credit include *Mogadishu, Minnesota* (HBO); *Our Girl* (BBC); Critical (Hat Trick Productions); *Savage* (BBC); *Postcode* (BBC/RDF Media), *The Journey is the Destination* (Prospero Pictures); *The Huntsman: Winter's War* (Universal Pictures); *Last Days on Mars* (Fantastic Films) and *My Brother the Devil* (Wild Horses).

ENGAGEMENT PARTNERS

The Claim was developed with the support of migrant organisations across the country, particularly in London, Stockton and Southampton. Through them, the play has engaged with hundreds of people with direct experience of the asylum system. The original tour included a programme of wraparound activity providing spaces for learning, reflection and action via free workshops, creative sessions, discussions and more, all co-designed with partners. Special thanks to following organisations:

GRAMnet aims to bring together researchers and practitioners, NGOs and policy makers working with migrants, refugees and asylum seekers. The network is currently funded by The University of Glasgow, whose academic community has a wide range of expertise in relation to these areas. The City of Glasgow is host to the largest population of refugees and asylum seekers under the dispersal policy as well as having a history of hosting large communities of migrants. The organisation is an internationally recognised research network that encourages interdisciplinary work. https://www.gla.ac.uk/research/az/gramnet/

Counterpoints Arts is a leading national organisation in the field of arts, migration and social change. Their mission is to support and produce the arts by and about migrants and refugees, seeking to ensure that their contributions are recognised and welcomed within British arts, history and culture. Central to that mission is belief in the ability of the arts to inspire social change and enhance inclusion & cultural integration of refugees & migrants. They work across all art forms and collaborate with a range of people and partners: artists, arts/cultural and educational organisations and civil society activists. They manage the Platforma network and Refugee Week. www.counterpointsarts.org.uk

Freedom From Torture is a national charity with a vision of a world free from torture. Its centres across the UK provide therapeutic support and expert medical assessments to support survivors' asylum claims, and uses its expertise and evidence to protect and promote survivors' rights and hold torturers to account. Its projects include Write to Life, the world's first creative writing group for survivors of torture. In the past 15 years, group members have written for online and print publications and developed and performed live theatre, music and film projects. www.freedomfromtorture.org

Queen Mary Legal Advice Centre (QMLAC) provide free legal advice to members of the public, staff and students at Queen Mary University of London. They act as a first-tier advice agency: providing preliminary advice on the strength of the client's case, the processes that need to be followed, and an explanation of complex legal issues. Clients come to the advice centre from a wide variety of backgrounds and present a wide range of legal issues. The award-winning Legal Advice Centre was opened by its Patron, Lord Goldsmith, in 2006. Since its opening, the Centre has advised over 1481 clients. http://www.lac.qmul.ac.uk

Right to Remain is a UK-based human rights organization. They work with communities, groups and organisations across the UK, providing information, resources, training and assistance to help people to establish their right to remain and to challenge injustice in the immigration and asylum system. www.righttoremain.org.uk

Ice and Fire explores human rights stories through performance, making accessible theatre for a wide range of audiences across the UK. With a distinct and determined voice, they develop original pieces from human rights testimony and documentary evidence. Each piece is shaped by real people and communities. From full-scale productions to smaller works with vulnerable groups, their theatre-making is renowned as provocative, principled and innovative. Their mission is to inspire artists and audiences to create positive change in the world through human rights.

The following organisations have also informed the play and its engagement activities in various ways:

Stockton Justice First, Open Door North East, Stockton Baptist Tabernacle, Southampton CLEAR, Refugee Action, Migrant Voice, The Refugee Council, Bards Without Borders, Detention Action, Migrants Rights Network, The Paper Project, Refugee Youth, Risky Things Theatre Company, Journeys Festival International, Volunteers Together, Herbet Smith Freehills Law Firm, Kanlungan Filipino Consortium, Garden Court Chambers, actREAL, COMPAS, Waging Peace, Rainbow Project, Good Chance Calais, Rise, Asylum Access, Bail for Immigration Detainees, Southwark Day Centre, SOAS Detainee Support, Border Crossings, Dash Arts, Cardboard Citizens, Beyond Borders, Cities For Sanctuary, A Moment's Peace, Citizens UK, Global Minorities Alliance, ingeus, Ketso, Pan Intercultural Arts, Citizens UK, Hackney Migrant Centre, Action for Refugees, Micro Rainbow International and Praxis.

Foreword

"I appreciate you speaking my language."

The Claim is made in a language I'd struggle to recognize as a mother tongue. Strange things are said by people talking in English yet passing each other like ships in the night. The world of asylum interview meets the world of a claimant, English is contorted and disported, mangled and tangled so that the right to claim asylum becomes unrecognizable as anything remotely close to what the origins of that word, in English, mean: 1. 'Shelter or protection from danger' 2. An institution for the care of people who are mentally ill. (OED).

As *The Claim* proceeds it becomes clear that language is not a shelter house for those in danger but a border where willful misunderstanding and monolingual mindsets win out. Language is not used in a way that cares for people in any state of distress. It truncates compassion and care, it twists like the snake pulled from the plastic packet of sweets, poisoning words which are trying to find safety, and slithering into oblivion.

In situations of distress language leaves us and becomes a cry, a shout of pain, breathlessness. Anne Carson, the poet, has spoken of 'the ancient struggle of breath against death'. The claimant 'remembers to breathe' and the life or death claustrophobia of language – straining for oxygen in the stifling world of the asylum process – is fully present on stage, stifling us all.

This is not verbatim theatre, it is imaginary and yet, as so often with the imagination, it fills us with the full horror of reality: what it means to claim asylum in 2017 in the United Kingdom. The playscript reads like so many six hour long transcripts of asylum interviews I have read, which have reminded me most of Absurdist Theatre. Such a system is held in place by political will, it does not occur by accident and it metes out its torturous punishing regime under cover of directives and the kind of excuses we associate with the Nuremberg Trials: "I was only doing my job."

Theatre offers a space in which our social iniquities can be gathered up and displayed in ways which offer a greater clarity. Working with Producer, Director and Playwright to enable this as a collaborative, careful, reflective venture is rare for a researcher. But it means, as someone whose role is to test and evidence and verify, I can read this script and say: "yes. This is true."

Professor Alison Phipps, UNESCO Chair in Refugee Integration
Through Languages and the Arts
(University of Glasgow)

Acknowledgements

Throughout development, the contribution of Mark Maughan has gone way beyond the traditional parameters of the Director's role. He has been there every step of the way, and the play would not exist without him.

Thanks are also due to many brilliant and kind helpers along the way.

To the performers who workshopped the play: Jaqueline Boatswain, Clifford Samuel, Christian Roe, Gemma Brockis, Jude Nwosu, Rosanna Miles, Robert Macpherson, Brian Ferguson, Angela Clerkin, Tonderai Munyevu, Elizabeth Chan.

To those who gave wise thoughts and guidance during its creation: Jessica Latowicki, Chris Thorpe, Deborah Pearson, Purni Morell, Ryan Craig, Gez Casey, Clare Foster, Malu Ansalu, Roz Coleman, Ric Watts, Hanna Streeter, Poppy Burton-Morgan, Nick Frankfort, Alex Ferris, Verity Quinn, James Grieve.

To those whose expertise grounded it in reality: Ben du Preez, Alison Phipps, Lisa Matthews, Tom Green, Lauren Roberts, Bella Hoogeveen, Katja Frimberger, Sheila Hayman, Shabab Hamid, Frances Ridout, Christine Bacon, Sharon Kanolik, Lily Einhorn, Stella Barnes, Rebecca Moore, Anne Stoltenberg, Ali Bandegani, Deborah Stanislawski, Laura Parker, David Jennings, Asha Mohamed, Bruce Goodison, Nazek Ramadan, Admir Selimovic.

To the true experts (by experience): those who eloquently and generously shared their own experiences of the asylum decision system with us. Michael, Brenda, Mustafa, Natacha, Jade, Aso, Conteh, Tracy, Prossy, Uganda, Hasani, Elif, Buba, Kate, all at Write To Life, and everyone else we met. We owe the most to you.

To my family, for all the years of everything.

To Jess, who makes me better.

This text went to press before the end of rehearsals so may differ slightly from the play as performed.

In loving memory of Gerald Asbury, 1930-2017.

So close.

First published in 2017 by Oberon Books Ltd
521 Caledonian Road, London N7 9RH
Tel: +44 (0) 20 7607 3637 / Fax: +44 (0) 20 7607 3629
e-mail: info@oberonbooks.com
www.oberonbooks.com

A catalogue record for this book is available from the British
Library.

PB ISBN: 9781786823908
E ISBN: 9781786823915

Characters

SERGE
male, Congolese, speaks French and
(quite limited) English

A
male, British, speaks English and
(fluently but not perfectly) French

B
female, British, speaks only English

The performers playing A and B should reflect
the diverse ethnic makeup of the UK.

NOTES ON PERFORMANCE

The performance takes place only partially in a fictional world occupied by characters. It never fully ceases to exist in whichever space it is performed in, occupied by performers and an audience. At times, the piece displays an awareness of this dual existence. Accordingly:

Time and space can be seen as both closed (continuous) and open (broken) across scenes.

Performers may remain visible to the audience when not in a scene.

Performers speak in their natural accents, even where syntax may suggest otherwise.

Performers speak to the audience – facing them and making eye contact with them – as well as to each other. The two forms of address are not mutually exclusive.

NOTES ON TEXT

The symbols $>$ and $<$ indicate the start and end of sections where it is particularly important that the audience is included, but these are by no means intended as the only moments of audience address.

The symbol ^ indicates a character's change of language within a single line. Switches in language that do not occur within a single line are not marked in the text.

The play was created with the intention that only one language is actually spoken on stage – ie changes in language occur within the fictional world and on the level of character.

A forward slash indicates overlapping dialogue: the slash marks the exact point at which the next line cuts in on the current one.

A dash in place of a character's speech indicates an active pause.

ONE

Houselights stay up. Stage lights not particularly theatrical.

SERGE enters. Some time. Eye contact.

SERGE: > I stand here sometimes and wonder what's
          expected.
          You know. What kind of act do they want?
          And what would happen if I was entirely myself?
          After all, this is a place of pretence. Yes?

          A enters.

A: Welcome.

SERGE: Thank you.

A: Are you comfortable?

SERGE: Well / I

A: I mean settling in.

SERGE: I appreciate you speaking my language

A: have you been here long? <

SERGE: I came here on holiday.

A: Did you?

SERGE: Well, officially

A: that's nice

SERGE: but it's not really a / holiday.

A: I need a holiday. Haven't had one for ages.

SERGE: I should explain.

A: Not since the summer anyway. Feels like ages.

SERGE: If I can put it into words

A: soon I am. I'm going to Ios.

SERGE: It's not easy to

A: do you know about Ios? <

SERGE: As you can imagine, I don't feel entirely / myself.

A: It's one of the islands, Ios. My partner told me to go.

SERGE: I wonder, do you have / water?

A: My partner! My esteemed colleague!

SERGE: Yes?

A: My friend, and compatriot.

SERGE: I'm sorry.

A: Why?

SERGE: You're busy.

A: No

SERGE: I don't mean to trouble you.

A: No /you're

SERGE: if I am – I can, you know

A: yes?

SERGE: Go

A: oh – please

SERGE: yes

A: don't be silly

SERGE: I'm not

A: no /it's –

SERGE: you think I / am?

A: It's an expression.

SERGE: Of course.

A: Yes?

SERGE: An expression.

A: Yes

SERGE: 'don't be silly'

A: 'don't be silly'

SERGE: 'don't be stupid'

A: there you go

SERGE: don't be a moron.

A: Well –

SERGE: moron!

A: Okay well that's a bit

SERGE: YOU MORON!

A: We don't really say that

SERGE: oh

A: no

SERGE: I'm sorry.

A: –

SERGE: –

A: So what's your. You know.

SERGE: Yes?

A: Story.

SERGE: My story.

A: Can I ask?

SERGE: Where to begin.

A: 'We'll begin at the beginning'

SERGE: yes

A: but I don't want to pry. And in fact we should / wait

SERGE: > So when I was ten years old, I mean of course I was born et cetera

A: we should wait for my partner

SERGE: but when I was ten I had this special piece / of gum.

A: I always remember stories. Sometimes more than real life! Sometimes I forget what I'm even doing in a room, do you get that? <

SERGE: Me?

A: Sorry, I'm just talking

SERGE: of course.

A: It happens. Like, when I'm nervous

SERGE: are you nervous?

A: No

SERGE: I get nervous

A: yeah I do a bit

SERGE: oh you do

A: I mean, I am.

SERGE: I see

A: yes

SERGE: so the opposite of what you just /said –

A: I didn't want to say so but, it's. Yes, I am.

SERGE: You wanted to pretend

A: to an extent

SERGE: that's how people are here

A: is it?

SERGE: This is a place of pretence

A: you shouldn't say that.

SERGE: –

A: –

SERGE: I think everybody's a bit nervous.

A: Nobody knows what's going to happen

SERGE: apart from you

A: and you

SERGE: not / me

A: and my partner of course. She knows.

SERGE: Your partner

A: yes

SERGE: so you have one

A: yes. Well sort of. She'll be along soon. You don't?

SERGE: Not at the moment

A: no, of course.

SERGE: Why of course?

A: –

SERGE: How do you say it? In your language

A: what?

SERGE: Partner

A: partner? It's – ^ partner.

SERGE: Partner?

A: Colleague, really

SERGE: 'friend and…compatriot'

A: that's just something I say.

SERGE: Because you're nervous.

A: > For me it's pressure, that makes me nervous.

SERGE: Yes, pressure sometimes gets too much

A: it's, responsibility, you know. Weighing down.

SERGE: All this pressure, on what you say

A: how accurate you are, or sound

SERGE: and what I have to say starts with my special piece / of gum

A: some people get numbed to it though, don't they? <

SERGE: You want me to say / this?

A: They stop feeling, to some extent just going through the motions.

SERGE: Yes, emotions /are a big factor

A: it's just a different approach

SERGE: they make it hard to say

A: I just like to feel it, always. For me that's the job, it's exhausting, but it's how I do my job.

SERGE: Your role

A: yes – sorry – now when you say 'role'

SERGE: yes

A: the word's gone completely out of my head. Come on! Role...

SERGE: role, like...part.

A: Part...

SERGE: to play

A: yes! I've got you. I am professional, it's just sometimes a word goes.

SERGE: Of course.

A: —

SERGE: I have to say – /It's –

A: can I do anything for you?

SERGE: It's difficult to talk when I'm /thirsty

A   here, if you're staying.

SERGE: Do you have a / drink

A: or, if you'd like to. Stay I mean. I'll take your coat

SERGE: please.

A: You don't need it in / here.

SERGE: please, I / would

A: I didn't mean to just leave you standing there!

SERGE: I would prefer / to

A: I'd like to help. Yes?

SERGE: No.

A: No?

SERGE: No

A: you'll keep it?

SERGE: Thank you.

A: For what?

SERGE: I'll keep it.

A: You don't want me to take it

SERGE: no

A: you'll be hot, won't you?

SERGE: Thank you very much.

A: –

SERGE: –

A: Suit yourself.

SERGE: Coat myself!

A: Sorry?

SERGE: Why?

A: –

SERGE: –

A: Oh. I see.

            I'm crap at jokes.

SERGE: So let me explain

A: no, I get it / now

SERGE: I mean my story

A: > we all love a story!

SERGE: My dad was reading me a book

A: that's why we're /here

SERGE: it was an English book, I think. The character's
            name sounded English: ^ 'Bucket'

A: it's amazing, the little details a mind can recall

SERGE: this particular night, he read to the end of chapter four

A: it's like who knows if they mean anything, these
            details, but they stick.

SERGE: He kisses me goodnight, he turns the light off, and
            he shuts the bedroom door.

A: Like that cartoon, 'Around the World in Eighty
            Days' – remember that?

SERGE: And I go straight to my drawer. I was only ten.

A: I must have been five, watching that, but it's in here
           (head) crystal clear.

SERGE: Maybe I was a stupid ten, trying to act like a
           character in a book.

A: He was a lion, the main character, and what was his
           name?

SERGE: It was a book about a chocolate factory

A: Willy!

SERGE: Yes, the man who owned the factory – he was /
           called Willy Wonka.

A: He was called Willy Fogg. Around the world in 80
           days, with Willy Fogg.

SERGE: See I loved this idea, the girl who keeps the single
           same piece, for months and months. <

A: Was there a girl?

SERGE: What?

A: I thought all the characters were animals.

SERGE: I wonder, is it possible to get / a drink?

A: He wore a top hat, didn't he? Top hat and tails. A
           little cartoon lion, in top hat and tails.

SERGE: –

A: –

SERGE: I'm disturbing you

A: no

SERGE: you have a story to tell

A: not me

SERGE: the lion

A: it's just a memory you know, bubbled up

SERGE: I don't want us to compete

A: I'm just passing time.

SERGE: I thought I must tell you this

A: well thank you

SERGE: but I haven't / yet

A: I imagine you'd like to sit down

SERGE: no

A: if you're sure

SERGE: but I am / thirsty.

A: He travelled in a hot air balloon. Can you imagine travelling like that?

SERGE: I never got beyond chapter four. That night – well, the next day…we left.

A: I'm just a curious person, I love other places.

SERGE: When I think back to how I behaved, I feel / shame

A: I'd love to hear about yours.

SERGE: Mine?

A: Where you're from, what's it like?

SERGE: Where I'm from?

A: Where you live?

SERGE: Streatham?

A: Really?

SERGE: –

A: I can't imagine an African version of Streatham. Is that bad?

SERGE: I don't / think I –

A: Are there animals?

SERGE: What?

A: I love elephants. Do you have those?

SERGE: Well, no.

A: Oh.

SERGE: I think if you go to the zoo you'll see them.

A: There's a zoo?

SERGE: You don't know London Zoo?

A: >I just really love elephants, I think they're magical.

I watched this programme where a group of elephants were on the move, and they came across the body of another. It was dead you know. 'Deceased'. Obviously, sad. They stood around, shuffling, they actually blew their trumpets a bit.

Trumpets? Not their trumpets. I didn't mean trumpets, I meant trunks!

SERGE: Elephants with trumpets!

A: I meant trunks.

SERGE laughs.

SERGE: The elephant brass section

A: yes

SERGE: the elephant jazz orchestra!

A: No – sorry – I'm telling a story.

SERGE: Of course.

A: They mourned it. The dead elephant. They trumpeted – I can say that – with their trunks, and they bowed their heads and they had, it's going to sound silly, but they actually had a minute's silence.

SERGE: –

A: Isn't that incredible?

SERGE: Yes

A: that's empathy.

SERGE: –

A: I probably watch too much TV though. I should read more books.

SERGE: Yes, so we finished chapter four, when the children were starting to / disappear.

A: Should be more like you

SERGE: You know the girl who disappears, the one who chewed the same piece of / gum

A: I started this crime series from the US recently. Bits I could hardly understand!

SERGE: Every day, for months, the exact same piece / of gum?

A: Yes, they kept saying 'piece', 'my piece' – eventually I realised they were saying it for 'gun'. <

SERGE: I became obsessed with this

A: with guns?

SERGE: So I kept my own piece of / gum.

A: Or with America, do you mean?

SERGE: I stuck it to the inside of my drawer. I wanted to keep it, like this character, this girl, as long as I could. And then after that night I said I would keep it until he came back.

A: Sorry?

SERGE: Why do you say 'sorry'?

A: Until who came back?

SERGE: Why do you say 'sorry' when you mean 'what'?

A: Why do you think 'piece' is slang for 'gun'?

SERGE: Anyway – he never came back.

A: Sorry, who didn't?

SERGE: My dad.

A: You lost him? Or he left?

SERGE: You could say that

A: well, / which?

SERGE: the next day, we left

A: you left him then – this is your holiday

SERGE: no.

A: I'll bet you've never been to Ios. Have you?

SERGE: –

A: Not many people have. Unless when they were a teenager like after A-levels but that's not really the same.

SERGE: –

A: It's okay if you don't want to talk right now, we can just wait quietly.

            Some time.

A: >My partner actually went. Ios. She went last year. So it was a direct recommendation, if you know what I mean!

            I was umming and ahhing, checking the flights every day. You know those doubts: is it my kind of place? Will I be bored? Will I find it, I don't know, tacky?

            In the end I thought 'just book it', it's just a holiday, you only live once. You have to reward yourself sometimes don't you? Just lie on a beach.

            And you know that feeling. That feeling's so good. To be able to sit here, and know it's coming. An escape. <

SERGE: I would really like a glass / of water

A: sorry, I'm doing it again

SERGE: please.

A: Tell me about yours.

SERGE: My what?

A   Your 'vacation'

SERGE: what vacation?

A: It means holiday

SERGE: I know

A: American

SERGE:	of course
A:	you said you came here for a holiday, you see.
SERGE:	Officially, a holiday
A:	but unofficially – what?
SERGE:	Unofficially, not.
A:	It'll probably be simpler if you just pick one.
SERGE:	Which one?
A:	If possible, of course, officially
SERGE:	if possible
A:	but really whichever is the truth
SERGE:	yes, I want to give truth
A:	that's why you're here
SERGE:	and you
A:	well it's a bit different for me, but you understand my motivation
SERGE:	–
A:	it's: I want to help. You're on my doorstep!
SERGE:	What doorstep?
A:	I'm not going to leave you shivering in the cold.
SERGE:	I'm not / shivering
A:	Thing is I can't just say stay, pull out the futon, there's a spare room, make /yourself at home –
SERGE:	there is?
A:	See it's not just me or I mean ultimately I'm not the one or at least I have to include my, on these things I defer to my, you know.
SERGE:	Yes?
A:	Partner.
SERGE:	I understand. I will just tell / you –
A:	but we'd like to hear your story, and then.

SERGE: I'm trying to tell you it

A: let's wait for her.

SERGE: I got a tourist visa

A: that makes sense

SERGE: yes, I paid, a man called Salim, it was the only way

A: most incontinent travellers I guess /need tourist visas –

SERGE: excuse me?

A: I said, most incontinent travellers / need –

SERGE: incontinent?

A: Is it – incontinence?

SERGE: no...I'm / not

A: incontinen-tal?

SERGE: –

A: –

SERGE: Do you mean intercontinental?

A: Exactly, intercontinental travellers is what I mean.

SERGE: Incontinent!

A: I'm not perfect

SERGE: no!

A: No one's perfect

SERGE: incontinent means when / you poo –

A: that's people it's humans, we're not

SERGE: I'm sorry

A: you were talking about your holiday, your visa

SERGE: yes

A: good

SERGE: okay

A: right

SERGE: so, it was never really a holiday.

A: Ah, yes, well I did assume that was…you know.

SERGE: Who would come here for a holiday?

A: It's not that / bad –

SERGE: So much rain!

A: Cornwall's got / some…

SERGE: listen / I –

A: cream teas.

SERGE: I have to admit. I / still don't –

A: what?

SERGE: –

A: What do you want to admit?

SERGE: No. I just. Still don't feel entirely – as you would say, myself.

A: You're not yourself

SERGE: yes, not myself.

A: Who are you then?

SERGE laughs.

SERGE: It's a funny thing to ask.

A: No but I didn't actually get your name.

SERGE: Who are you!

SERGE laughing.

A: But actually though.
What is it? Your name.
Stop laughing.

SERGE: I am…Mr incontinent!

SERGE laughing.

A: Stop now.

SERGE: Incontinent!

A: Stop it. It's not funny.

SERGE laughing.

STOP, okay, will you stop laughing at me.

SERGE stops.

What's your name?

SERGE: Serge.
My name is Serge.

Some time.

A: I didn't mean to raise my voice.

SERGE: It's okay.

A: Did I raise my voice?

SERGE: I don't think / so

A: it's unprofessional, I'm sorry.

SERGE feels his pockets and finds a little bag of pick n' mix gummy snakes.

SERGE: I think I'll have a snake.

A: I read an article. It said concentrate on your breathing.

A concentrates on his breathing. Some time.

SERGE: Would you like a snake?

A: Sorry?

SERGE: A snake.

A: I don't know what you.

SERGE: Yes?

A: You mean a snack?

SERGE takes a snake from the bag.

SERGE: I love snakes.
Would you like one?

A: –

SERGE: –

A: I'd – yes, please.

         SERGE gives A a snake and they both eat.

         Thanks.

SERGE: Friend.

A: –

SERGE: You're my friend. Now.

A: That's nice. I'd like to be.

SERGE: You're kind.

A: I'm just doing what any decent, you know, my job

SERGE: I know how it is, you're very busy, I come along

A: it's part and / parcel!

SERGE: you weren't expecting it

A: no, I was. That's it you see, I was.

SERGE: You were?

A: We were.

         B enters.

TWO

House lights slightly dimmer. Stage lighting slightly more theatrical.

A: > hello

B: hello.

A: This is my partner.

B: My colleague

A: my partner and my colleague!

B   My colleague. We're professional. This is just our job. *(re. SERGE.)* Who's this?

A: *(Not registering B's question.)* My esteemed colleague!

B: Just say co-worker

A: friend and com /patriot

B: just co-worker will / do.

A: okay. <

          Some time.

B: What are you eating?

A: Snake.

B: Why have you got a snake?

A: –

SERGE: –

B: Has he got one too?

A: Uhhh no. Yep.

SERGE: Yes?

B: Do you think that's appropriate?

A: To what?

SERGE: Would you like a snake?

A: Do you want one?

B: –

A: –

SERGE:	–
B:	...yep.

A gets snake from SERGE. Gives it to B.

SERGE:	Hello
B:	hello.
SERGE:	Everybody likes snakes
B:	yes. Although, is that true?
SERGE:	What?
A:	That's not, necessarily, per say, true
B:	just because, some people actually hate them.
A:	I guess some people have a phobia
SERGE:	but they are so very good
A:	they are good.

Some time.

B:	Sorry, I don't think we were introduced.
SERGE:	–
B:	What's your name? What's his name?
A:	/Serge
SERGE:	Sese.
B:	–
A:	–
SERGE:	Yes, / Serge.
A:	I thought his name was Serge.
B:	Sorry. What did you say, just then?
SERGE:	Hello.
B:	Hi.
SERGE:	Please for meet you
B:	yes, and you. Please, sit
SERGE:	yes?

B: Don't put yourself out

A: she prefers it if people just relax

B: can I ask, what name did you say just then?

SERGE: –

B: What name?

SERGE: Serge

B: no before, you / said

SERGE: I use the name Serge

A: he uses Serge

B: I don't think you said that / though

A: I think you said another / name

SERGE: I also have the name Sese.

B: Sorry?

A: Sese.

B: Okay.

A: It's a second name, maybe?

SERGE: Sese is my name, but I use the name Serge.

A: Have you got a headache?

B: I'm just tired

A: have some water

B: I don't want water

SERGE: yes? Please

A: you need a holiday

B: everyone would like a holiday

A: I'm having one soon

B: yes, I'm aware.

A: Ios, remember? Your recommendation

B: no, I know

A: I said we should go together

B: well that was a joke

A: it wasn't a / joke

SERGE: excuse me?

B: Do you want to hang your coat up?

A: He actually / said he'd

B: your coat? Shall I take that?

SERGE: No. No.

A: He wants to keep it on

B: he'll be hot.

A: Do you think he can stay?

B: It depends

A: of course

B: you know it depends

A: listen, between you and me –

B: don't be silly

A: 'don't be a moron!'

B: What?

A: No, just something he said.

SERGE: Yes?

B: Yes he called you one didn't he

A: well no – I mean, sort of

B: did he threaten you?

A: No

B: you look a bit shaken.

A: I'm fine

SERGE: if you like, I can go.

A: No – ^ look, okay. Don't make a big deal, but I wanted to pass this on. I do think he might have been sleeping…you know.

B: What?

A: You know

B: no

A: rough?

SERGE: Excusing / me –

B: you think he might have been sleeping rough.

A: Don't say anything though.

B: What makes you think that?

A: Sometimes you just get a sort of feeling. But let's not say anything.

B: Have you been sleeping rough?

SERGE: What?

A: We don't need to / ask

SERGE: rough?

B: I'm sorry, but he said you had

SERGE: –

B: I'm just trying to find out how we can best help, so I would like to know.

A: Have you been sleeping on the – on the street?

SERGE: I've been staying in Streatham.

B: Streatham?

A: On the common?

SERGE: Near the common

A: but in the street

SERGE: the street is Margolis Road, and before that, Ballards / Road

A: So – yes / it seems like he has.

SERGE: My number: 9, 3, C.

B: In Streatham?

A: Near the common

B: but on the / street

SERGE: Streatham is nice.

          B smiles at SERGE. A concentrates on his breathing.

B: Right. Well we should probably get a bit more information.

SERGE: Yes?

B: I'd like to, if that's okay? Because we have a little don't we

SERGE: please, slowly

B: but not enough.

          A, eyes closed, concentrating on his breathing.

SERGE: I am – not enough?

B: Don't worry. It's just me wanting to know one or two things. Establish some basics. Would that be alright?

SERGE: Thank you.

          A exhales long and deep.

B: What are you doing?

A: Concentrating on my breathing.

B: If he was abusive to you then / we can have –

A: no he wasn't abusive

B: verbal abuse is still / abuse

A: I think it was a joke

B: you're acting weird. Look at you

A: I'm just breathing. It's a technique

B: well if that's what you need to do for a bit, then fine, but please do it elsewhere

A: what's that?

B: I can manage

A: can you?

B: I am. Aren't I? *(To SERGE.)* aren't we.

SERGE: Aunty?

B: See?

A: I'm not sure / that's

B: you go and do your, whatever / you're –

A: he's much more comfortable in French

B: do your thing, get yourself together

A: I am together

B: you're the opposite of together

SERGE: she acts like your mother!

A: No she doesn't

SERGE: I think so

A: no – / I –

SERGE: yes!

A: Hey, okay look Serge, I'm actually trying / to *help*

B: come on, you're raising your voice

A: I don't want to raise my voice

B: I know you don't.

        A closes his eyes. Breaths deep.

B: I'll handle things, okay? Just for a bit.

        A exhales.

THREE

Houselights dimming slowly. Stage light slowly becoming more theatrical.

B: So.

SERGE: So.

B: –

SERGE: You are the… partner

B: oh please, don't you start

SERGE: excuse – speaking slowly

B: no just the partner thing, don't start

SERGE: I start?

B: No, don't start

SERGE rummages in his pocket.

SERGE: start is, I have ten years old. My father /read this book.

B: Sorry – what are / you –

SERGE: I tell you?

B: What have you got in there?

SERGE: My story – / it's hard –

B: Do you think you could just take your hand out?

SERGE pulls out the empty bag that contained the gummy snakes.

SERGE: I think there are more.

B: Right.

SERGE: But, not more.

B: Are you diabetic?

SERGE: Diabetic?

B: Are those for that?

SERGE: Excuse. I want to have / water

B: please let me know if there's anything like that.

SERGE: It is…possible?

B: What is?

SERGE: I give you – last one.

B: Thank you.

SERGE: Welcome.

B: Shall we put that away now though?

SERGE: Candy.

B: Sorry?

SERGE: Always sorry!

B: Sorry / I –

SERGE: British.

B: I'd like to ask you a couple of /questions

SERGE: > you always say sorry. But most often, you don't mean sorry. <

B: If we could just / sit –

SERGE: > I saw a man who walked into a lamppost and he said sorry to it. To the lamppost! <

B: Hello?

SERGE: Hello.

B: Sorry, what was that?

SERGE: Yes?

B: You were just talking.

SERGE: Talking

B: What were you talking about? Just then.

SERGE: Candy?

B: Right. Could we – could we try to speak the same language?

SERGE: Yes?

B: Please?

SERGE: In America, you say – candy

B: but we say sweets

SERGE: 'sweets'

B: you should sit down. Make yourself comfortable

SERGE: you have nice eyes

B: excuse me?

SERGE: Nice eyes.

B: –

SERGE: –

B: I would really very much like you to sit.

SERGE: Sit?

B: Please

SERGE: thank you. I don't want.

B: Well, yes okay, but this isn't all entirely about you.
            I mean of course, it is. It *is.*

SERGE: What 'is'?

B: I just want to help. To understand.

SERGE: We don't, I think. Understand

B: yes, well if you sit / down

SERGE: I think I must – to go

B: here, please, be my guest.

SERGE: Guest?

B: Okay?
            Sit down for a minute.
            Please, sit.
            Rest your feet.
            SERGE sits.
            There we go.

SERGE: I sit five minute. Here.

B: Yes, or maybe a bit more.

SERGE: Please, / a drink

B: you can see this as a sort of a preliminary

,SERGE: –

B: we'll go into more detail at a later stage. Okay?

SERGE: –

B: Now, so far today I think you've made a couple of claims.

SERGE: Claims?

B: Yes

SERGE: this 'claims'

B: yes, exactly

SERGE: is shellfish?

B: Selfish?

SERGE: This bad / for me.

B: Well it's not selfish if it's genuine.

SERGE: I can not eat.

B: I assume you're not saying it isn't genuine?

SERGE: How do you say…allergic. I don't know the word

B: I mean that would be somewhat self– /defeating

SERGE: I'm still learning. ^ I learn, yes? Now.

B: Yes – do stay in English, if you can, please.

SERGE: Is not easy.

B: So you've made one or two claims

SERGE: I think we not / talk

B: for example about elephants

SERGE: you have / drink?

B: and I think America, and holidays, and – is this right? – guns

SERGE: listen –

B: well *I'm* talking / now

SERGE: I can phone, someone / come

B: please do relax.

            SERGE gets his phone out.

SERGE: I make / phone

B: I know it's not the / comfiest.

SERGE: I call somebody, she can / come

B: Sesese, listen, I think there's a little confusion.

SERGE: Maybe she is free. My friend. She / take me

B: sorry, can I have that? Please? Can I?

SERGE: You?

B: Yes please.

SERGE: Why?

B: If you just put it there. That's it. Just there.

            SERGE places phone down. B picks it up.

            I want to have a chat. It would make me happy if we could.

            Just a quick one really, and we can start to get to the bottom of this.

SERGE: Bottom?

B: Is it okay if I keep this?

SERGE: Please, give me.

B: It's just one of the rules.

SERGE: I cannot lose.

B: Everybody has rules, don't they. Have you ever been into a house without rules? For example shoes off, that's a rule, in some people's houses, or in a mosque.

SERGE: –

B: Isn't it. Sesese? Some places, you take shoes off.

29

SERGE: –

B: Don't you, sometimes? Take off your shoes?

SERGE starts taking his shoes off.

B: No, not here. Okay. No, keep those on. Sesese. Don't, please.

>That's not a rule we have here. But no one's allowed one of these, not turned on at least, not even us really, and we're here every day!

SERGE: Please.

B: I'll put it here, okay.

SERGE: No, I ask, no.

B: We don't want trouble, do we, some inquest, you know what people are like, so we have to stick to the, what's the word, the protocol. Yes?

SERGE: –

B: Usually there's an announcement about these. *(indicates phone)*

SERGE: I don't /under –

B: it's just to say, it's a fixed process really, this. You see? Fixed.

SERGE: Fixed.

B: People say oh I bet every day's different, what you do, I bet you never get bored, well no actually that's not so, is it? Because it's the same old rigmarole. Did I say rigmarole? Or is it protocol. Are they the same thing? But I'm going off on one. You get into a groove, a pattern, is what I'm saying, so to speak. <

SERGE: Your partner. I / would like

B: I really – I do not have a partner

SERGE: yes.

B: No.

SERGE: You – lie

B: Me?

SERGE: Yes

B: –

SERGE: –

B: Are you sure you're comfortable? In your coat? Be
          honest. I'd be very happy to take it.

SERGE: No.

B: I don't want you to be uncomfortable, so if you
          want something, you tell me.

SERGE: I want / water

B: so I'm going to ask you about your journey here.
          Now, where did you start?

SERGE: Start is, Willy Wonka.

B: Sorry?

SERGE: I have ten years. My father he reads to me / and
          then he –

B: where have you come from? Can you tell me,
          where you come from?

SERGE: From?

B: Where are you from?

SERGE: From…Streatham

B: that's just where you've been sleeping

SERGE: slipping?

B: on the street.

SERGE: Yes: Margolis Road

B: but where are you actually from?

SERGE: Nine three C. My house.

B: I don't think so

SERGE: I think so

B: because if that's where you're actually from

SERGE: yes

B: I mean truly from, well that would mean you'd have, for example, a British passport.

SERGE: Yes. Okay. I tell you: real life. No passport.

B: You don't have a British Passport.

SERGE: No.

B: Right. I didn't think so

SERGE: very bad.

B: What passport do you have?

SERGE: No passport.

B: You don't have a passport at all. Any kind.

SERGE: You have passport?

B: Of course

SERGE: you are...lucky

B: no, I'm just British

SERGE: yes.

B: –

SERGE: –

B: How did you get to Streatham, is what I'm asking. How did you travel?

SERGE: Travel – Oyster.

B: Sorry?

SERGE: Oyster Card.

B: Before you were in Streatham. Before you were in England.

SERGE: Oyster shellfish also?

B: No – / I don't

SERGE: is funny name.

B: Now, Sesese: I'm / trying to

SERGE: please – you say Serge.

B: sorry?

SERGE: You, call me. Serge.

B: But your real name is Sesese

SERGE: Sese, or Serge. First name: Sese. Not Sesese. One
         two. Se, se

B: I'd prefer if you didn't patronise / me

SERGE: is not one two three, is one two: se se.

B: This is quite important.

SERGE: But – you call me / Serge.

B: Sese, okay – did I say it right? Now: before
         Streatham. Before that. Where were you?

SERGE: Is simple name.

B: What's your nationality? What country are you
         from?

SERGE: Country?

B: Your country.

SERGE: My country is Congo. But – long time.

B: Good.

SERGE: Not good. Very bad.

B: Democractic Republic of Congo, or the other /
         Congo

SERGE: yes

B: which?

SERGE: What?

B: Are you from DRC? Democratic Republic? / Or

SERGE: yes!

B: Okay. And when did you come here?

SERGE: Today?

B: You came to this country today?

SERGE: Yes?

B: I'm trying to find out when you arrived. You arrived, first time? From DRC?

SERGE: I arrive aeroplane.

B: Right, good, but when?

SERGE: Visa say, holiday.

B: But it's not actually a holiday is it… as I think you said.

SERGE: I have to say 'return flight twenty-two June'.

B: What do you mean 'have to say'?

SERGE: He write it, for me. Salim.

B: Who's Salim?

SERGE: This only way…I can come.

B: So – shall we say June? That's when you came?

SERGE: Or, is – maybe – July.

B: Can you not remember the month?

SERGE: I come – June July, twenty… six ten.[1]*

B: Twenty *sixteen*?

SERGE: Twenty sixteen.

B: Right.
           Twenty sixteen.

SERGE: Two thousand… sixteen

B: two thousand and sixteen

SERGE: this is different way to say

B: no, I know.

           Some time.

B: And why is it you don't want to go back to Congo?

SERGE: Want?

B: Yes

---

1   * These dates correspond to the play's first production in November 2017. Dates should be adapted so that months named are no more than 3-4 months prior to the current production, and the year named is always the previous year. So for example a production in April 2019 could adapt to January or February, 2018.

SERGE:	is not 'want'
B:	why not?
SERGE:	Please, I tell / him.
B:	You can go to Congo? Now?
SERGE:	No
B:	why?
SERGE:	I am afrightened.
B:	What are you frightened of?
SERGE:	–
B:	–
SERGE:	I am ten years.
B:	Well that would make you a child.
SERGE:	My father reads for me.
B:	You're obviously not a child.
SERGE:	He goes, light close.
B:	I would like to put your actual age.
SERGE:	But I want to be…not sleep. In my bed, yes? But not sleep. Just me, my gum.
B:	Yes you mentioned that, didn't you, before. This is something that happened in Congo?
SERGE:	This Congo, yes.
B:	And you said 'my', so – you had your own firearm?
SERGE:	I not sleep. I hear. Very bad things. ^ How do you say gunshots? And screams. ^ 'Bang, bang.' Yes?
B:	Bang bang. That's a gun?
SERGE:	Yes
B:	So I'll just put, you left because of an incident with a firearm? Something like that?
SERGE:	Is long time. But hard to speak. I feel shame.
B:	I understand

SERGE: no understand

B: but if you tell the truth now, it will be much better for you later. So please do think about this carefully: have you been involved in any kind of illegal activity?

SERGE: I know only what I…sound.

B: Smuggling, for example? Maybe of arms?

SERGE: I do not know who comes, my house, this night. Their name.

B: Or were you maybe part of a militia?

SERGE: Militia, yes. I think

B: you were involved / with a militia?

SERGE: I do not know, but I think, maybe is M23 – he comes.

B: M23, that's a militia, in Congo, is that right?

SERGE: Sorry. Is hard.

B: We're nearly done. I just want to establish a timeframe.

SERGE: –

B: So – this incident, with the firearm? It was a long time ago.

SERGE: Yes?

B: You said 'Long time'

SERGE: yes, long time.

B: So now, it's safe? For you, in Congo? Because time has passed? Congo is safe?

SERGE: No, no. Please. I think, they do…they kill me, there.

B: How much time exactly has passed?

SERGE: Time?

B: Yes, how much time?

SERGE: I don't have – time.

B: Five years?

SERGE: I have time, my phone.

B: Ten?

SERGE: You give me?

B: Sese, I'm simply asking how much time passed, between then, when this incident occurred, and now.

SERGE: I don't understand, you. Your language, my language, bad.

B: Okay.

SERGE: Okay?

B: Let's just try one more

SERGE: no more

B: can you just tell me why it is that we're only doing this now?

SERGE: –

B: Why you didn't come to us sooner? For example, in June 2016.

SERGE: I don't speak at you

B: yes, just tell me this last / thing

SERGE: I speak at your partner

B: my colleague

SERGE: my friend

B: or co-worker, if you like

SERGE: I tell him my voice, my language, my words. What happen for me. Yes?

B: Is that what you want?

SERGE: this, I want.

B: So you're requesting him?

SERGE: I don't speak you.

B: So, we'll use him, of course.

SERGE: Give me, my / phone.

B: I'm making a note of your request.

SERGE: Please.

B: But I do need you to answer this last question / first.

SERGE: I cannot lose.

B: 2016, you arrived. Yes?

SERGE: Yes, I tell you.

B: But why didn't you come here? In June 2016

SERGE: yes, as I say!

B: But you didn't come specifically here. To *us*. You should have come straight away.

SERGE: –

B: Why didn't you come to us?

SERGE: –

B: I need you to say something here. Please.
         Sese, June 2016. Why – you – don't – come – here?

SERGE: I don't come, because I fear this.

B: What?

SERGE: I am fear about you. What you think of me.

B: Me?

SERGE: You.

B: But I don't think anything of you.

SERGE: This my fear.

If SERGE moves or exits, he doesn't entirely do so of his own accord.

FOUR

Houselights dimmer still. Stage lights becoming quite theatrical.

A: > Hello

B: hello

A: my partner

B: you have to stop saying that now

A: but it's true

B: we work together

A: we do stuff together

B: just work

A: and stuff

B: we don't do 'stuff'

A: we could. <

B: –

A: I was looking at the flights

B: what flights

A: to Ios. They're still cheap.

B: I'm not coming to Ios with you

A: but you loved it / there.

B: Can we please just say co-worker, okay, from now on?

A: If we were in a cop drama you'd be my partner

B: we're not in a cop drama

A: if we were in *Beverley Hills Cop*

B: we're not in that

A: *Starsky and Hutch. NYPD Blue. The Wire.* I could go on.

B: Please don't.

A: But we'll say colleagues

B: co-workers

A: if that's what you like.

B: It's not what I like it's just what it is

A: you can be very empirical

B: you don't even know what that means

A: I do.

        Some time.

B: Listen, I think I should tell you something. About Ios.

A: I'm counting down the days!

B: I think I should tell you about an event, that sort of happened when I was there.

A: She really did love it. She was so relaxed, when she came back

B: but listen /when I was –

A: normally I tend to be more...adventurous.

B: What's that supposed to mean?

A: It's just who I am

B: what are you saying?

A: Nothing, just.

B: I always go to places like Ios.

A: I know

B: calm waters. Guaranteed sun

A: of course, all that's lovely and I'm going now, and that's great

B: so stop complaining

A: I'm not complaining. I'm just saying, one thing I'm aware of is anyone can go to Ios.

B: No they can't.

A: It's not even another continent.

B: It's Greece

A: it's an island

B: so it's *off* Greece

A: I'm just saying normally, I'd be looking for more adventure

B: what does that mean, what's an adventure?

A: I dunno

B: you mean the kind of place you can't drink from the tap don't you

A: no

B: that's what you mean. Reverse snobbery. You think somewhere like Ios is a bit first world

A: don't

B: what?

A: say 'first world' /you shouldn't –

B: I'm just saying, you're more interested in... other worlds

A: okay so what if I am interested in 'other worlds'

B: like Mars

A: well, not like Mars

B: Mars is another world

A: you're taking the piss out of me

B: –

A: > I *would* go to Mars, though, if I could. If people, I mean, could

B: but they can't

A: there's not even any water there at all

B: well except there is <

A: there isn't

B: yeah, they just found it

A: when?

B: I don't know. Like, last year[2]*

A: did they?

B: It was in the news

A: Fuck.

B: Yeah

A: fuck me. That's amazing.
        Because, you know, where there's water, as they say

B: what?

A: Where there's water, there's life

B: –

A: as the saying goes.

B: Would you listen to yourself

A: why?

B: Just listen to yourself

A: I can't listen to myself actually, it's impossible to
        talk and listen at once.

B: Do you want to hear it? What happened to me?

A: I'm all ears.

B: Because I think you should.

A: Please.

B: So I was driving along the road.

A: Beautiful. The open road.

B: Shut up and listen now

A: she likes to boss me about, it's how we / are.

B: > I had a hire car. You get a hire car, don't you?
        You can't rely on public transport in a place like
        that.

---

2   This can be changed to reflect roughly the time passed since water was discov-
    ered on Mars (2015).

I'm driving along the coast road. I'm on my way to a beach. The beach is called Manganari beach, it's one of the quiet ones.

So I come around a bend on my way there, and as I come round the bend I see this motorbike. I see this motorbike just lying there, in the road. Obviously I stop, otherwise I'll literally, so to speak, smash right into it. And as I come to a stop, I see that there's also a guy lying there. He's lying a couple of metres away from the bike, on the edge of the road, and he's not wearing a helmet and he's lying there on the tarmac and immediately I'm thinking: fucking fuck, he's dead.

I'm just characterising a little bit for you – that's the voice I had in my head. Fucking fuck you know: a dead body.

I kneel down to look at him, to see I suppose if he's alive. And as I do, I hear an engine revving. And when I look round, I realise it's my engine. It's the engine of my car. And there's a man behind the wheel, and he just drives off. Not fast, or anything. He just eases the car around me, around the motorbike, the guy in the road, and he just drives off along the coast. <

A: Wow. That's really.

B: –

A: I guess, at least it wasn't your actual car

B: it had my passport in it. It had my phone.

A: What about the motorbike guy. Was he dead?

B: No

A: well that's good

B: is it?

A: Isn't it?

B: He was in on it, he must have been. I watched him get up, almost straight away, as if he'd woken up, you know, from a nap, and just get right back on his bike. He didn't speak English, or pretended not to. I was shocked for a moment you know but then I was shouting at him: what about my car! You bastard! You racist, you sexist bastard! That was pent up frustration from the past few days, that, because do you know what it's like to go on holiday in a place like that, if you look like me?

A: I don't

B: no you wouldn't

A: no, I don't.

B: I mean I still loved it, the place, the weather, the sea, but you do just feel a bit examined, you know. A curiosity, or a piece of. And then for that to happen.

A: I can only imagine

B: but you can imagine.

A: –

B: –

A: You said Ios was a lovely place

B: it was, apart from that.

A: You said it was amazing

B: it was

A: it's quite a big detail to leave out.

B: I had travel insurance. The embassy helped me, you know. I actually upgraded my phone, when I came back.

A: But you don't expect that on holiday. You don't expect that kind of treatment, that kind of scam.

B: Although in some ways of course you do

A: do you?

B: It's a phrase, isn't it, 'holiday scam'

A: holiday scam, yes. Holiday scum.

B: Don't say that

A: why not?

B: It's racist

A: against who?

Some time.

A: > Once a woman stopped me on the corner by where I live. She told me this long story about how she'd been locked out of her house. She said she needed to get to school to pick up her son, but she couldn't get the car keys or her phone or even any money, because she was locked out. She was frantic. Her eyes were crazy, you know. Well, I could imagine what that must be like, your kid waiting by the school gates, all alone. We all make mistakes.

B: Human error

A: I gave her a tenner. She needed a taxi you see, to get her son. She was desperate.

B: You were kind.

A: But it bugged me. I thought, why do you need a taxi to pick him up?

A few days later she rings my doorbell. You know, the threshold of my actual house. Same story. Exactly the same. I said I'm sorry but I'm not that stupid and she kept going on about it not bashful at all not scared, just jabbering no shame and in the end I told her to actually fuck off, I used those words, fuck off, I said fuck off now. Probably three or four times. I said it through gritted teeth you know almost a snarl, 'fuck off'. 'Fuck off'. Fuck off!

And I shut the door. <

Some time.

45

B: Sometimes you have to

A: I felt bad though

B: she tricked you

A: she was desperate

B: the world's problems can't all fall at your door.

A: You mean feet

B: I mean door

A: but what if they do?

B: They can't, or how do you live?

A: What if there's a reason why they do?

B: No.

A: I just feel… responsibility

B: you do your job. That's responsibility. You do the best you can, what you're told, you turn up, early if possible and at least on time, and you try to smile.

A: You don't smile

B: I do sometimes

A: not often

B: it's not a prerequisite.

        Some time.

A: Can I say something?

B: Free country

A: I like him.

B: Who?

A: What do you mean who?

B: I mean who. Who do you like?

A: Serge?

B: *(Remembering.)* …oh yeah.

A: —

B: –

A: And he likes me.

B: okay

A: what?

B: No, nothing

A: what?

B: No it's just I think that's, it's a nice idea

A: but?

B: Well you know.

A: No?

B: It might not be the case

A: why not?

B: You're a – because you're a means

A: I'm not a means

B: a means to an end

A: I'm not. I'm an end if anything, to my own means

B: what does that mean? How can you be an end to your own means?

A: Although sometimes I think we're all a means without an end.

B: I'm just going to ignore that

A: why?

B: Look I would just say, if it was me, I wouldn't be trying to be his friend.

A: He's nice.

B: This stuff about guns. And the M23

A: what, the motorway?

B: Do you not know about the M23?

A: I know it skirts Maidenhead

B: it's a militia

A: right

B: Also, he's been abusive to you

A: no he / wasn't –

B: he's actually lied about being on holiday, and about his name

A: well that wasn't a lie / per se

B: and then it emerges he came here from Congo well over a year ago. Assuming we believe Congo is really where he's from.

A: Which we do

B: because did you notice what he said about elephants?

A: What – he likes them?

B: He said there aren't any there.

A: Where?

B: Congo

A: right

B: –

A: what?

B: Well, I just think…there are.

A: Shall we check?

B: Okay

A: is it okay?

B: Well, why not?

A: I guess, the / rules

B: look on your phone, it's important.

A: Is it?

B: Go on.

A checks on his phone.

A: Oh. No.

B: Are there?

A: That's really sad.

B: What?

A: They're being massacred

B: who are?

A: '68 elephants massacred in 60 days'

B: massacred? In Congo?

A: Look.

A shows B the phone.

That's more than an elephant a day.

B: What are they being massacred for? For their tusks?

A: Poor things.

B: Where does it say?

A: Look 'massacred', famous forest elephants of Garamba, massacred, you see that word? that word is 'massacred'.

B: But they haven't been massacred entirely though. There's still lots of them left

A: well, some

B: and it does say 'famous'. They're actually famous, these particular elephants

A: or what's left of them.

B: We should get back to it. Yes?

A: I suppose it could just mean the elephant, as an animal, is famous.

B: –

A: Probably not though. It probably means those elephants specifically.

B: > They're amazing animals

A: they're my favourite

B: I mean – if your country had them, you would know.

A: Well *I* would

B: of course you would

A: but I guess – maybe not everyone's like me

B: it's just basic fact-checking.

A: I mean do you ever worry about being a bit self-absorbed?

B: That's something that always astounds me

A: people are the same though, aren't they

B: because even if you're going to lie

A: fundamentally

B: it wouldn't take much to get a fact like that straight.

A: But is that true to life?

B: What is 'true to life'?

A: Well life's – it's complicated

B: we're not really in the business of being true to life

A: right.

B: –

A: Sorry, I thought we were in the business of that.

B: No

A: what are we in the business of, again?

B: We're in the business of coherence

A: right

B: we're in the business of consistency

A: yes

B: we're in the business, when it comes down to it, of credibility

A: credibility, yes. Incredible

B: what?

A: The way you come out with those words, just like that

B: I've learnt them, it's my job

A: sometimes I look around – and this is probably one of those moments – and I think wow you know, I am *surrounded* by incredible people

B: we really should press on

A: I bet this place is full of incredible people, just under this one roof

B: shall we press on?

A: Serge is incredible, I reckon

B: yes, he probably is.

A: It's people, is what I think. People are incredible. <

B: Okay?

A: Listen, that story I told.

B: Can this wait?

A: It wasn't strictly you know, true. I mean it was true, it just didn't actually happen to me.

B: –

A: It happened to my mum. When I was growing up.

B: Okay

A: but is it okay?

B: Well, whatever

A: you told one, and then I wanted to, and it seemed to work, rhythmically or – I don't know

B: you were just passing time

A: but it wasn't my story. And I embellished it

B: we all embellish now and then.

A: Did you? With yours?

B: A little bit

A: do you not feel bad about it?

B: Why should I feel bad about it?

A: –

B: It's only a story.

          If SERGE moves or enters, he doesn't do it of his own accord.

FIVE

Houselights dimming at last to nothing. Stage lights reaching their most theatrical.

B: I've brought someone to see you.

A: She's brought someone to see you

SERGE: who's she brought?

A: Who've you brought?

B: I've brought you

A: she's brought me

SERGE: I see.

A: Your friend.

SERGE: –

B: Will you explain to him?

A: What?

SERGE: Did you bring / water?

B: How we're going to do this

A: yes. ^ You remember, you said new friends.

SERGE: That was a long time ago

A: very funny

SERGE: it's not a joke.

A: –

SERGE: –

B: You understand?

A: She says do you understand?

SERGE: Understand what?

A: No, sorry, I was meant to. So, it's language

SERGE: what about it

A: that's why I'm / here.

B: we haven't got loads of time.

A: She wants to get started

SERGE: I thought we already did.

A: It's just the schedule, there are targets, times, that
        we have to, even the building itself has to, you see

SERGE: see what?

A: People have to go home et cetera so it's not
        personal. It's not about you.

B: I'd like to start now

A: I mean, of course it is, it is, about you.

SERGE: –

A: I like you. I want you to know that

SERGE: funny

A: no – / I

SERGE: yes

B: what's he say?

A: Nothing.

B: He obviously said something

A: he says I'm funny

B: funny?

A: Yes

B: you?

A: Yes

B: no you're not.

A: –

SERGE: –

B: So let's make a start

A: she's going to ask you questions, I'll interpret them

SERGE: you mean translate

A: we say interpret

SERGE:	an interpretation
A:	yes
SERGE:	like a version.
B:	Okay? Are you comfortable? I want you to be comfortable
A:	are you cozy?
SERGE:	Cozy?
A:	Comfy
SERGE:	no
B:	yes?
A:	You should take off your coat
SERGE:	please stop saying that
B:	I want you to feel that you can say anything, here. Just the simple truth, in your own words, your language – we thought you'd be more comfortable you see. Well indeed you asked. We're trying to accommodate you so please do try to relax, and just answer in response to my questions.
A:	Err – okay so, she says, I want you to feel the freedom to say anything
SERGE:	I don't feel freedom
A:	to say only the straightforward truth
SERGE:	so do I say nothing?
A:	In your words, with your tongue, we had thought you were comfortable, that's the accommodation we try to provide so do relax and make your answers a reflex to my questions.
SERGE:	What?
A:	Did that not make sense?
B:	I'm assuming you do understand, at this point, why you're here?
A:	Do you know now why you're here?

SERGE: Of course.

A: Of course

SERGE: because you're keeping me / here

A: well, no, you came of your own / volition

SERGE: it's about you, yes? Not me

A: it's about both, it's you telling us

SERGE: telling you what?

A: Your story

B: is there a problem?

A: Or at this stage, substantiating it, as we say.

B: Now, I will ask you more about your involvement with this militia and so forth. But first, I'd like to hear a bit more from you about your country, and your circumstances there.

A: She will ask you to go into detail about the militia – yes?

SERGE: What?

A: But first she's going to ask you to confirm some things about Congo.

SERGE: To tell you the truth – / I haven't

A: exactly, it's a chance to do that

SERGE: right, well if / you listen

A: and to start with, to prove Congo is in truth where you're from.

B: Okay?

SERGE: So the truth is that I have not been in Congo for many, many years.

A: –

B: Yes?

A: Sorry. ^ Sorry, can you. Just repeat that?

SERGE: I was in Uganda before I came to your country.

56

A: Why didn't you say so before?

SERGE: I didn't have the chance

A: it's going to look bad

B: what's going on?

A: he – he says – I was in Uganda, before here. I haven't been in Congo for several years

B: sorry – he hasn't been in Congo?

A: Apparently

B: for how many years did you say? for several?

A: For several

B: how many is several?

A: How many is several?

SERGE: Several?

A: How many years would several be?

SERGE: Why?

A: She wants to know

SERGE: well it's unspecified, that's why it exists

A: what?

SERGE: As a word.

A: Can you give me a number though?

SERGE: What do you think?

A: It doesn't matter what I think

SERGE: but you said / it.

A: *(To B.)* He doesn't seem sure

B: right.

SERGE: Is it maybe – five?

A: He says…maybe five

B: 'maybe five' – see that's not very precise

A: that's not all that precise

SERGE:	no, exactly
A:	precisely, no.
SERGE:	Look.
A:	He says 'look'
SERGE:	they wanted to send me back. This is the Ugandan police. They would often come – tell her – to threaten us, they beat my / uncle –
A:	they wanted to send me / back –
SERGE:	why are you interrupting?
B:	Who did?
A:	I'm interpreting
B:	who wanted to send you back?
A:	The Ugandan police
B:	to where?
SERGE:	I tell him, your partner – I get money, many years
B:	Sese / please
SERGE:	make chance to come. Tourist visa, passport, all this.
B:	Sese, listen, I need you to stay in French
SERGE:	then arrive, London, Salim take my passport
B:	please don't speak English / now
SERGE:	no more / passport.
A:	Speak to me.
SERGE:	*(To A.)* My visa said I was here on holiday, you understand? I told them a family wedding. I was told to tell them that. But it wasn't real
A:	I wouldn't say 'it wasn't real'
SERGE:	but that's the story
A:	stick to what is real for / now
B:	can you include me?
A:	–

SERGE: So tell her

A: I don't think I should

SERGE: then I'll speak for myself

A: but we know that doesn't / work

SERGE: I can not rest Uganda, yes? I can not rest Congo. Here, I can rest.

B: Sesese, please. It needs to be: I ask a question, he translates it, you answer

A: try to just be yourself

SERGE: I am just my words.

B: That way I can find out everything I need to about your story, with minimum fuss

A: she wants to interrogate your story, in an efficient way, and it needs to all / line up

SERGE: why 'interrogate'?

A: and I'll facilitate / that.

SERGE: I haven't done anything

B: Is that clear? You're here so we can make sure we understand why you're here.

SERGE: I haven't done anything wrong. Everything I have done was to just try to live

B: what's that?

A: He's – he's saying he doesn't understand why he has to undergo this kind of questioning, because he hasn't done anything wrong

SERGE: I live here now, I don't harm anybody – this is the way I live

A: he's living here, not harming people, all he's trying to do is live a certain way

B: is that why you're here? To live a certain way?

A: Did you come here for a certain kind of lifestyle?

SERGE: If you call not being threatened a lifestyle.

A: Uh – no, it's not about lifestyle

B: Is that his word, lifestyle?

A: Did you say lifestyle or did I?

SERGE: I haven't done anything.

B: Yes?

A: I'm innocent

B: innocent of what?

A: What are you innocent of?

SERGE: I don't know.

A: I think he's confused. Maybe he hasn't eaten very / much

SERGE: please ask her for / water

A: I feel bad, that we ate your snakes.

SERGE: Okay. Listen. I'll / explain

B: so where were we?

SERGE: In Uganda, they wanted me to go back to Congo, / but how can I?

B: Please wait for my questions. I'll ask specific / questions

A: wait for her questions

SERGE: you have to tell her the whole / story

A: I don't know the /whole story

B: it can't just be / anarchy –

SERGE: I just want to explain

A: he just wants to / explain –

B: can you ask him to look at me rather than you

A: she needs you to look at her, and we will answer her questions

SERGE: but she isn't asking me about my story.

A: He wants to tell his side of the story

B: of course

A: we'll hear your side of the story, in due course

SERGE: what side?

A: Your side.

SERGE: It's not / a *side*

B: but for now I do need to insist that you wait for my questions, and when they come, simply answer them, and don't ask your own.

A: Okay. We will just answer her questions. Don't ask questions – that's her job.

B: Okay?

A: Just say okay.

SERGE: Okay.

B: Everyone okay?

A: Okay.

B: Okay then.

A: –

B: –

SERGE: –

B: So, firstly.

A: First question.

SERGE: I'm extremely thirsty

B: firstly, can you tell me about the wildlife in the Congo.

A: She'd like you to tell her about the animals in Congo

SERGE: the people?

A: The animals

SERGE: I have danger in people. Not animal.

B:	Okay – but I'm asking about wildlife
A:	she's asking about animals, not people
SERGE:	why?
A:	He doesn't know why you're asking
B:	please answer the question.
SERGE:	It's a stupid question
A:	you just have to try to be consistent
SERGE:	with what?
B:	Hello?
A:	With everything.
SERGE:	Gorillas.
A:	–
B:	Yes?
A:	They have…gorillas.
SERGE:	Isn't that exciting. Gorilla safari. Just drive off up into the hills, it's very fun in my country.
A:	That's sarcasm isn't it
SERGE:	What do you think?
A:	…yep, gorillas they're known for.
B:	Is that all he said?
A:	…yep.
B:	What about elephants?
A:	Do you have elephants?
SERGE:	Elephants?
A:	Elephants. Do you have those?
SERGE:	Yes, I think so.
A:	Yes
SERGE:	aren't we lucky.
B:	Yes?

A: He thinks so

B: so he's saying yes, now?

SERGE: Yes, elephants, / yes!

B: please stay in your language

A: use me.

B: Previously you said you didn't have elephants.
      Didn't you.

A: Before you said you don't have elephants

SERGE: in Congo?

A: Yes. You said it to me.

SERGE: I didn't say that.

A: You did

SERGE: no. You asked me about Streatham

A: elephants, in Streatham?

B: Is he denying he said it?

A: Everybody knows there aren't elephants in
      Streatham

SERGE: but you asked

B: I have to insist /I'm kept in the –

A: the only elephants in London are at London Zoo

SERGE: I know!

A: He's talking about Streatham

B: I'm not asking about Streatham

A: no, I know.

B: Now Sesese

A: it's Sese, two / syllables

B: Sese, sorry, I am trying / to –

A: but he does prefer / Serge

B: Sese, okay: now, which part of the country are you
      saying you lived in?

A: Where did you live back home?

SERGE: In Uganda?

A: In Uganda?

B: Is Uganda your home?

A: Would you call Uganda home?

SERGE: No, not really

A: no

B: so, where is your home?

A: Where would you call home?

SERGE: Streatham

A: apart from Streatham. It's going to be somewhere in DRC

SERGE: originally, I'm from the east of DRC

A: okay, so – Eastern DRC.

SERGE: The region was South Kivu. My family had a house. But I haven't lived there for some time, because as I told you I was in Uganda.

A: The South Kivu region. South Kivu?

SERGE: Yes

B: South Kivu?

A: Yes

B: isn't that an area that's now secure?

A: She says she thinks it's now secure

SERGE: how does she know?

A: It's – material. Files

SERGE: what material?

A: Reports.

SERGE: Have you been there?

B: Yes?

A: He wants to know if you've been

B: I just want to do my job, I don't want to discuss everything

A: she doesn't want to discuss that.

SERGE: You go in Congo? You go there?

B: No, Sese, okay. No. I have not been there. Okay?

A: She hasn't

SERGE: so she doesn't know

A: I'd actually like to go to that part of / the world.

B: Can we continue?

SERGE: I can't go back. I really can't.

A: I can't go back.

B: Why? What exactly happened?

A: Why can't you?

SERGE: My uncle went back. Before I came here.

A: My uncle went before I came here

SERGE: he went from Uganda to Congo, and he disappeared. So I can't say it's safe.

A: his uncle went, from Uganda back to DRC, and disappeared

B: okay

A: which shows him it's not safe.

B: Sese –

A: Serge –

B: Do you have proof that your uncle disappeared?

A: Do you have proof of your uncle's death?

SERGE: When people want to hide something, there is no proof.

A: When people want to hide something, there is no proof

B: those are his words?

65

A: those are his words.

B: –

A: –

B: What is he hiding, then?

A: I don't know – I'm not sure that's what he meant.

B: Do you have any proof at all? Documents, letters, websites maybe with your name say on a list or something. Anything like that?

A: Do you have any proof of what has happened to you? Like letters or online / materials

SERGE: we left in a rush. I was young. In Uganda we weren't official.

A: So you don't have any proof?

SERGE: I am proof.

B: Does he?

A: ...no.

B: And what reason are you giving for going to Uganda, initially?

A: Why did you go to Uganda at the initial moment?

SERGE: Because of my dad.

A: Because he left you

SERGE: he didn't *choose* – I've been trying to say this.

A: He went because of his dad

SERGE: I am ten years old, he tells me a story / and then –

B: does his dad live in Uganda?

SERGE: It's hard to speak of. I told you. I feel shame.

A: It's hard to say – I think something bad happened, when he was younger – he's ashamed

B: of what? Is this the incident with the gun?

SERGE: In the morning, my mum says 'what other option do we have?' And we went across the border.

A: In the morning they went across the border. ^ So something happened the previous night?

SERGE: There were supposed to be cousins in New Jersey, but we / were rushing, no time

B: New Jersey, did he say

A: yes

B: New Jersey, America?

SERGE: It was very fast.

A: Something happened that night, yes, that means you can't go back?

SERGE: Yes.

B: Well?

SERGE: –

A: This is hard.

B: Yes, it is.

A: No I meant – for him.

B: Does he want a minute?

A: Do you want a moment?

SERGE: Please.

               Some time.

A: I'm still going to go, you know

B: what?

A: To Ios

B: let's not talk about that /now

A: despite what you said. I'm not scared.

B: America keeps coming up. Doesn't it.

SERGE: I'm sorry.

A: You're ready?

SERGE: So, this night. / I was –

A: she says America keeps surfacing.

SERGE:	What?
A:	America. Surfacing?
B:	Has he ever been?
A:	Have you been at all?
SERGE:	No
A:	no
B:	you understand that if we find you had been there, it would affect the likelihood of you staying here.
A:	Are you sure you didn't make any claims there?
SERGE:	What / claims?
B:	can you explain how you know words like vacation? Like candy, and 'piece'?
A:	How do you know the words vacation, candy and 'piece'?
SERGE:	American is common, from TV
A:	from TV
B:	I thought he was more into books?
SERGE:	I will die. Okay? If I go back, I'll die.
A:	He's quite anxious, because he believes if he goes back he'll die.
B:	Yes we've established that, but I want to know exactly *why*
A:	why will you die? Who do you think killed your uncle?
SERGE:	I don't even know he's dead
A:	so he might be / alive?
B:	What does he say?
A:	I'm asking him about his uncle, to explain the links
B:	please don't advise him
A:	if you want to cry, you can cry

SERGE: what?

A: It would be appropriate

B: Sese. If you don't tell us why you believe you'll die, it's impossible for us to help.

A: If you don't tell her, she can't help you

SERGE: I've been trying to tell you from / the start

A: I think he's working up the courage

SERGE: I am just a person. An ordinary person. Everybody like stories, but you can't always be the wonderful story that you like.

A: Just tell us the story of that night

SERGE: I am.

B: Yes?

A: Okay…we all like a good story…but it's not always possible to be one

B: we don't need a story, we just need the truth

A: don't tell a story, tell the truth

SERGE: I was a child. I had stupid ideas, obsessions. I had a piece just this one particular piece / of gum

A: yes so he was a child, he had stupid ideas, fixations, and he had this 'piece'

B: can we just say gun now?

SERGE: It became a sort of charm for me. My piece. It made me feel safe or strong.

A: His piece – sorry, gun – it was an object that made him feel strong, like a charm

SERGE: I kept it stuck to the inside of a drawer, because I was trying to live up to a story. Willy Wonka. I told you before.

A: He kept it inside a drawer…he was trying to be like Willy Wonka

B: is this a joke, about Willy Wonka?

SERGE: I know it's stupid, but it explains what I did that night

A: no, Willy Wonka, it's linked to that night

B: the night he fled?

A: The night you fled?

SERGE: We left in the morning, this is the night before.

A: They fled in the morning, but yes the night before.

SERGE: My dad reads me the story. He turns off the light. I take my piece from the drawer – and then I don't know what happened. I'm just scared, all this noise, I sit in my bed

A: yes?

SERGE: Do you know the sound of the gunshots, very close?

A: Me? No, I – Sorry – ^ Do you know the sound of gunshots, close up

B: not personally

A: I think it's a rhetorical question. ^ Are you okay?

SERGE: It was a long time ago. But the shame.

B: So is he saying he actually fired the / gun?

A: It was a long time ago but I'm ashamed.

SERGE: I was just a child

A: I was a child.

B: A child with a gun

A: well, yes

B: so, what, a child soldier?

A: A child soldier?

SERGE: What?

A: Weren't you?

SERGE: No

A: apparently / not

SERGE: you have to understand, even at the time, I knew, this was a stupid thing

A: you mean dangerous?

SERGE: I wouldn't say dangerous

A: but wrong?

SERGE: More or less

B: yes?

SERGE: I told nobody, it was my secret piece of /gum

A: so – I knew it was wrong: I told nobody, it was a secret gun

B: he hid it in a drawer, yes?

A: You kept it secret in a drawer?

SERGE: Yes.

A: Yes.

B: Because…?

A: Why?

SERGE: Because my mum wouldn't have approved

A: my mum wouldn't have approved

B: only his mum? What about his dad?

A: Just your mum? Not your dad?

SERGE: Is that important?

A: Every detail is important

SERGE: well it was different with my dad

A: it was different with his dad

B: his dad wouldn't mind about a firearm, but his mum would

A: more or less

B: so at least someone had their head screwed on

A: at least your mum's head was directly attached

SERGE: what?

B: So this stuff about the sound of the gun going off,
        close up.

A: Yes

B: he shot someone then? And it was the last time he
        saw his father – did he shoot his own father? Is that
        it?

A: Were you defending yourself? Someone came into
        your room, and you thought they were attacking
        you

SERGE: my dad wanted me to be special

A: yes, right – I'm sorry – was it your / dad?

SERGE: He always said, every day, what kind of person do
        you want to be? You can be someone, you can be
        special.

A: His dad was every day coaching him, to make him
        a certain kind of person

B: what kind of person?

A: What did your dad want you to be?

SERGE: Special

A: special

B: special forces?

A: Do they have special forces there?

B: Ask?

SERGE: That was my moment to show who I was, and I
        showed: I'm not special.

A: But your dad was?

SERGE: Yes.

A: Yes, it seems so

B: snd he was coaching you to do what? use a gun?

A: Did your dad teach you to use a gun?

SERGE: A gun?

A: Yes

SERGE: did yours?

A: It's not about me

SERGE: I don't see what it's relevant to

A: well, to everything.

B: –

A: –

SERGE: There are noises, okay, outside the door.

A: There's noise outside the door. *(To SERGE.)* The bedroom door?

SERGE: Yes

A: the bedroom door.

SERGE: I don't understand the noise. I'm hiding in the covers, crouching, ready

A: I'm hiding in the sheets, I'm ready, but I don't understand the noise

B: what is the noise?

SERGE: I don't move. I don't get up from my bed, I just wait, and I still hear this screaming, now. It's inside my head

A: I – so – I don't move, I don't get up from the bed, I wait, I hide. I still hear the screams.

B: Screams?

A: Yes

B: that's the noise?

SERGE: And then BANG.

A: Yes it's screaming he hears and then just...BANG.

SERGE: In the morning, my dad is gone. That was the end of him for me, there.

A: And then, in the morning, his dad is gone – it was the end of him.

B: So he ended him?

A: Who ended who?

SERGE: What?

B: That was the end of him, because you used your gun?

A: Did you use your 'piece'? That night?

SERGE: As I said, I took it, I chewed it

A: you mean used it

SERGE: if you like

A: yes, he used it

B: he fired it

SERGE: I should have done something else, but I was young.

A: I should have acted differently but I was so young.

SERGE: I should have opened the door, gone out there. I didn't even get off the bed.

A: He didn't open the door. He didn't even get off the bed. Just shot through it I guess

B: well don't guess. What door? The bedroom door?

A: You're talking about the bedroom door?

SERGE: Yes.

A: Yes, like I thought, which means he couldn't see

B: okay.

A: So it was basically an accident.

SERGE: So much shame.

A: But he feels ashamed.

B: Because of his part in it?

A: Because of the role you played?

SERGE: Maybe I could have done something

A: you mean something different

SERGE: I mean anything at all

A: but you did do something

SERGE: no. Relying on superstition is not / something

A: I mean you did something…huge

SERGE: me?

A: You regret it, of course you do.

SERGE: What do you mean, huge?

A: It's painful, clearly, and he wishes he'd acted
          differently.

B: And you're saying immediately after this, you fled
          to Uganda?

A: After that night, you went to Uganda?

SERGE: The next day

A: the next day.

B: And stayed there until coming here

A: yes.

B: So you think you are wanted, in DRC? Is that it?
          For what you did?

A: Do you think you're wanted in DRC? for what you
          did?

SERGE: I told you, my shame is that I did nothing

A: Serge – it's not 'nothing'.

SERGE: Why are you saying that?

A: Because it's the opposite

SERGE: what do you mean?

B: Yes?

A: Look – you caused someone to – you shot someone.

SERGE: What?

A: And not just anyone.

SERGE: Hold on –

A: your own dad.

SERGE: Why are you saying that?

B: Hello?

A: Because, I know it's horrible, and it wasn't your / fault

SERGE: what are you / talking about

A: but if it happened, it's not nothing.

B: Sese, should I put that you're wanted?

SERGE: No. No. Wait.

A: I think you're a victim, it was the situation, I don't think you're a bad / person

SERGE: no no no no no

B: I would like to begin to wrap up soon.

A: She wants to know if you think you're / wanted

SERGE: okay, just wait – listen to me.

A: He says listen, and / wait

SERGE: you have to cross that out, cross it completely / out

A: you have to cross it out

SERGE: I didn't shoot him.

B: Cross what out?

SERGE: Why would I shoot him? How?

A: I told her it was an / accident

SERGE: this is why you asked about a gun?

B: I want to know / who he's wanted by.

SERGE: Why you said that about my dad, teaching me, to use a gun?

B: Is it the state? The police?

A: Are you wanted by / the police –

SERGE: I didn't shoot him. I never said that. Someone else was shooting.

A: I didn't shoot him, someone else did.

B: Are you changing your story?

A: Are you changing your story?

SERGE: No you are changing it

A: I'm not, it's not mine to / change

SERGE: I already told you, I just heard the sounds. They were outside the door.

A: I think it's trauma

B: what is?

A: What do they call it? Disassociating.

SERGE: I was ten years old, of course / it wasn't me –

A: Serge, I understand, you had this huge / trauma –

SERGE: cross it out. Okay? Yes?

A: He's still saying he wants it crossed out.

B: Sese, we can't just cross out something like that.

A: She can't cross out something like that

B: what I'll do, okay, is make a note that you said this

A: but she'll make a note you said this

SERGE: said what?

A: Said what?

B: 'Cross it out'

A: she'll make a note you said 'cross it out.'

SERGE: –

A: –

SERGE: What else have you told her?

B: We have to finish in a minute / okay

A: we have to finish soon.

SERGE takes B's hand.

SERGE: Please. This bad. Help me.

B: Sese. *(To A.)* Okay, this is bad. Help me.

SERGE: I don't know what he / say.

A: Serge –

B: okay really, just get / him off –

SERGE: what he say / about me?

A: Serge, please

B: get him off me / right now

SERGE: I am not bad, I am /scared.

A: Serge, you're not / allowed

B: get someone! / Just get someone

SERGE: you want me to be special / but I am normal

B: security – I want / security

A: okay let's / all just

B: press the security / button!

A: No it's okay. Serge! Stop it. Serge. Get off. Get off.
         Off her.
         That's it.
         Okay.

         SERGE's stops holding B's hand.

B: Fucking hell

A: you can't touch her

B: you can't touch me, okay. That's against the rules.

A: She says you can't touch her. There are rules about
         that.

B: Jesus

A: okay?

SERGE: –

B: –

A: –

B: I think we're about done.

SERGE: I am just a person

A: I'm just a person

B: yes you keep saying that

A: you're repeating yourself.

Some time.

A: Listen. I've been thinking.

SERGE: I'm not the victim, or the villain, you want / me to be

A: *(To B.)* you're exhausted.

SERGE: But you want me to / pretend

A: *(To B.)* it's been crazy.

B: What did he just / say?

SERGE: To act

A: *(To B.)* All this, every day, round and round, the words. It's self-care.

B: What?

A: *(To B.)* Just come with me

SERGE: I'm not who you want me to be

B: *(To A, re. SERGE.)* is this important?

A: *(To B.)* Come with me to Ios

B: I'm not coming with you / to Ios

SERGE: not what you want to hear, or see

A: *(To B.)* I'll book your ticket, alright? I'll hire the car. I'll drive, /I'll –

B: stop talking about it, okay, for fuck's sake, I do not want to come with you to Ios, okay!

A: –

SERGE: –

B: –

B stands.

B: I don't have any more questions.

SERGE: The problem is the need to pretend.

A: She says we're done.

B: Does he have any last statements?

SERGE: Did you tell her?

A: He's very keen for you to understand that the problem is pretending.

SERGE: You understand?

B: Yes I think I understand

SERGE: yes?

A: Yes

SERGE: she understands?

B: I completely agree with you on that

A: she agrees

SERGE: she agrees?

A: She agrees with you on that

SERGE: big problem

B: yes. Very big.

A: We all agree

SERGE: …good.

A: No, it's not / good.

SERGE: so it's clear we should start afresh.

A: It doesn't work like that.

B: Goodbye, Sese. We'll be in touch.

B exits.

SERGE: Where's she going?

A: We have to stop now.

Some time.

SERGE: I never finished the story.

A: –

SERGE: I think it would have been incredible.

A: –

SERGE: A whole river of chocolate, it had in it.

A: …yes.

SERGE: You prefer the other.

A: What other?

SERGE: The hot air balloon.

A: Willy Fogg.

SERGE: My story is the wrong story for you.

A: I'm sorry.

SERGE: You're finished as well?

A: Yes.

SERGE: And me?

A: –

SERGE: I'm finished?

A: Well. I don't. I can't.

SERGE: She has gone home

A: in effect

SERGE: everyone is going home.

A: More or less.

SERGE: Is anyone going back to Streatham?

A: –

SERGE: Perhaps I can have a lift

A: I don't think so.

SERGE: What am I supposed to do?

A: –

SERGE: Just sit?

A: Try to relax

SERGE: when it's over

A: it's almost over.

SERGE: No.

A: You'll get a letter.

SERGE: Why are you saying that?

A: That's how it works.

A stands.

SERGE: I have a life, you know.

A: I've got to go.

SERGE: I have friends. I have a / house

A: > Thank you.

SERGE: It's not 'my' house as in, I don't own it, but I live /
there

A: thanks for your time

SERGE: I live at 93C Margolis Road. My room is at the back
of the house. Outside the window there's a garden
with a small tree.

A: Okay.

SERGE: Sometimes when I get back from work and climb
into bed, there are birds singing in the tree, even
while it's still dark. <

A: That's a nice image.

SERGE: –

A: But you don't need to be ashamed

SERGE: of what?

A: Sleeping on the…streets.

SERGE: You haven't listened.

A: That's my job.

SERGE: You said every detail is important.

A: I meant details of your journey, your escape

SERGE: no escape

A: not of your life here. Or these kind of, well…
fantasies.

SERGE: I thought it would be different here.

     Some time.

A: Can I get you anything else? Before I go.

SERGE: –

A: –

SERGE: Water.

A: Water?

SERGE: Water

A: just some water?

SERGE: Yes, water.

A: Of course.

SERGE: It's not difficult.

A: No it's – not at all.

     A gets SERGE water.

     We've got it on tap!

     Sorry. That was a. Sort of. Joke.

SERGE: –

A: Please.

     A hands SERGE water.

     SERGE slowly brings the water to his lips.

     He starts to drink. He drinks for some time.

     By the time SERGE is finished drinking, A is gone.

     *SERGE sits with the audience. Eye contact. As long as
possible.*

     END.